GONE AWAY

Phil & Kay!
Twins like
"islands"!

love
Maryann
7/17/07

Books and CD by Mervyn Taylor

An Island of His Own (New York & Tucson: Junction Press, 1992)

The Goat (San Diego: Junction Press, 1999)

Road Clear, CD, Mervyn Taylor (poems) & David Williams (bass) (Brooklyn: Goat Productions 2004)

Mervyn Taylor was born in Port of Spain, Trinidad, in 1941. He moved to the United States as a student in 1964, completing a degree in English at Howard University in 1968 and an MFA at the Columbia University School of the Arts in 1981. For more than thirty years he was a teacher of English and Creative Writing, first at Bronx Community College, then in the New York public school system and at the New School. He has been the recipient of three New York State Arts Council grants. His work has been included in numerous anthologies.

Currently, Taylor divides his time between New York and Trinidad. In both places, he is an avid participant in Carnival, the many faces of which often appear in his work.

MERVYN TAYLOR

Gone Away

JUNCTION PRESS
NEW YORK
2006

Some of these poems have been published
in the journals *Poetry International*, *St. Ann's
Review*, *American Letters & Commentary*, and
Rattapallax, and in the anthologies *Chance
of a Ghost: an Anthology of Contemporary
Ghost Poems*, *Palpable Clock—25 years of Mul-
berry Poets*, and *Bum Rush The Page*.

Cover art by Bruce Chandler.

Junction Press, PO Box F, New York NY
10034

for my grandson
Julian

CONTENTS

I. Crossing Streets

Crossing Streets

for Mervyn Lewis

This is the corner where our friend stood
before they said he had died suddenly
on Wednesday, and we kept repeating,
But we saw him just last night.

This is where the tree stood that became
infested with borers, and left a dust like what
covers the floor in a woodworker's shop,
and the city men came with saws that chopped
and whirred and we could count the naked rings.

This is how the arguments continued, night
after night, while the lady in the SRO fretted
about the ruckus, about what we do in the name
of culture, one man's music being another man's
noise, the beating of oil drums in the night.

This is the room where he succumbed
to heart failure, his mother going blind back
in the island where he'd left her alone for a minute,
his green card in jeopardy, a little pull on the reefer
his one vice. Pag, we called him,

because he could swim like the fish.
This is the bowl in which we observe each other
crossing streets, recalling the ocean
between here and home, hearing a mother
stumbling in the dark, calling, my son, my son.

The Name

The name of the city
says what it is, how it funnels
smoke on cold days, how it reels
under bright sunlight.

The name of the street whispers
its winding way, its small oaks
braced with rubber and wire,
the faces of its addresses.

The man's name lets him
answer with pride or
embarrassment, makes him
accused or popular.

Called out in court
or across the street, the name
stretches the banner that
bellies and gulps the wind.

Brownstones

They make the neighborhood solid,
yours recognizable for the flowerboxes
and the stained glass window your sister
brought, when she moved back in.

Your father nods in the sunlight slanting
across the living room. In the garden
are the beds he planted when he first
moved here from Guyana, many years ago.

The banisters are worn, the stairs
creak as workmen hammer on the floors
above. There is dust everywhere, even
in the blanket covering his knees. In his

stories, he stands behind the counter
of a pharmacy in Georgetown, a precise man
who now casually wears mismatched socks
and refuses to use a hearing aid.

He prefers the shouts and lean-ins
of his wife and daughters as they move
about the house, reminding him who
this is, the new tenant, and

this, the grand-daughter's new husband.
You, as the middle child, have the job
of holding his hand, and bringing him
back to the sea-wall,

the point at which he left off telling
his tale, his eyes shining with mischief,
as if he knew all along where every brick
was, having put it there himself.

Dream House

for Hilda

Every Friday she goes
and watches the new house,
how the foundation is laid,
how it seems it will never get done.

She says a prayer. Here,
a door will open wide
for the furniture to fit, for a visitor
to come in. Her daughter will wake
on a Saturday in that corner room.

How it haunts her, this dream
of a house: the cement, the bricks,
the lumber, the workmen, feet up,
smoking and chatting in
her living room.

The Super's Son

The super's son's all grown up now.
He sports a mannish beard
and gives me surly looks since
his old man and I had that run-in.
He bounces the ball hard
in the space between the garbage cans
and the back of the building.
On Tuesday nights he helps his father,
the heavy black plastic bags
slung to the sidewalk out front
with an attitude, the way men
who do hard work make us others
get out of the way.

Ghost Driver

He waits for a customer who never appears.
The base often sends him on these crazy
wild goose chases all over the city.
In this neighborhood he has been robbed
repeatedly, has the mark where the barrel
was the last time pressed against his temple.
He doesn't remember the gun going off
but ever since drives through a twilight
of wrong addresses and bad pickups, teenagers
who bolt without paying, cops who ticket him
for expired insurance and tarnished medallion.

He never runs out of gas, and he sleeps in his cab
at the side of the road. Mavis his shotgun rider
has long since abandoned him. Only yesterday
he noticed her makeup mirror still on the shade.
This fare is not coming. He sighs, makes a U and
listens to the lilt of the West Indian dispatcher,
asking if anyone is near Ditmas and 23rd, anyone,
anyone? Apparently not hearing over the crackle
as he answers, I am, I am, I am....

The Monarch

A butterfly swims among the plants
in my house. It is a monarch that
must have followed me home.

The fan of the elephant ear opens,
the butterfly goes in and out,
the croton and the ivy grow excited,

like children. I must think fast,
the day is getting older by the minute,
and this species is fatally sensitive to cold.

Sunstroke

Everybody's headed for Florida.
Hot as it is, it's the closest thing
to island weather. Their hearts still
long for home, but they've been away
too long: the old streets are too narrow,
buses break down, and they've become
used to conveniences, hospitals
that operate, lawmen who respond.

They know the state is directly
in the path of every hurricane,
and that lightning once struck
six people sitting on a fence.
But they figure Carnival is close
enough, and the water is warm,
though there's not a mountain to
look down from. And the men on
death row don't black out the city
when their time comes.

Sunshine State

A crazy woman ran across the highway
last night. She did a nervous skip once
she gained the grassy verge, and stood
in the glare of the lights, staring.

We drove on, swinging by large estates
with high walls, reflector lights turning
trees blue, the acreage sloping down
to plastic ducks in the man-made lakes,

and came finally into the quiet lane that
backs the house. But I couldn't get her out of
my mind, the woman against a huge dark sky,
with nothing to keep her from disappearing.

Noon In Dakar

She sends pictures that show
the wonderful plumage of birds
that come to her garden, where

she sits among them, adjusting
her beads, wrapping and tucking
the ends of her brilliant bou-bou

in place. By the time blackbirds line
the wires of avenues in Brooklyn
giving their shrill wake-up call

it is already Friday in Dakar,
a day for serious dressing-up.
She's long dressed, and gone.

Magenta Lake

for Moon

In Senegal is the lake
that grows pink in season,
when the villagers come
for salt.

By April their hands
are dyed
like an initiate's
going to fulfill his pledge.

You sit at the edge
of this body of water, purple
as the mark of his manhood
you try to soothe.

Train on a String

How far from home she is,
the African woman who calls
the cable car to Roosevelt Island
the train on a string.

It looks like it will fall,
hanging above the river.
She takes the bus instead
to get to the lady she looks after.

The car sways in the wind
as it goes across. The people
read their newspapers calmly,
or look out the windows.

But she, back home,
would go for miles up-country
where the lions hunt, rather than
travel in such a contraption.

She sings the old Kikuyu songs
her grandmother taught her, and
braids the lady's hair
a different way each day.

The Park

Because you haven't climbed
in a long time the hill is a killer.
You need a curb to mount, you
and your short legs, so funny.
Coming down the steep trail,
you catch things in your mouth,
until the ground levels and you forget
to pedal. Someone suggests a rope.

We stop to rest, my left foot
falling asleep on a curve of the lake
where the ducks come right up
in pairs, two white, two brown,
and you show me where the hair
is coming back after yesterday's wax.
Surprisingly your helmet fits me.
I didn't know it was the law.

A woman in Moslem black kicks
a white ball against the landscape
of trees and clear sky. It is a most
memorable picture, her children
almost forgotten in the privacy
of her play. Some days are ours,
however we choose to spend them.
Whatever the vendor charges for
the cones, we pay it, gladly.

And get back on our bikes, gingerly,
sex not being the subject of the day,
except in the distended belly of a bird
as her mate feeds her, in the drake's
splashing in the wake of the female.
All else is breeze, and encouragement,
as if the world is just learning to walk again,
a homeless man thanking God for summertime.

23

Between Belmont and Brooklyn

Uttering an exclamation, turning
to avoid the unseasonable cold,
I feel the warmth of the doorstep
where I left the dog blinking in the sun.

I'm back, I tell my neighbors,
though it seems they didn't know
I had gone. I touch one of the new
spring-red tulips by the park. It shivers.

There must be some sign that
I went away—longer hair, darker skin,
slower manner of speaking. Imagine,
the block burned down...No,

that happened before I left. I left
something in the yard there too,
where the crotons do their tricky calypso,
the one plant the bugs leave alone.

Gone Away

Four years turned into forty.
I missed my mother's funeral,
the Black Power uprising,
the thighs of an old woman
that became a lifelong dream.

The mountains turned brown
and green that many times,
the savannah too. The lane
grew empty, while I searched
for love in the metropolis,
turning back at the borders,

my papers in disorder
in a trunk in Brooklyn.
I wrote letters that turned
into poems, cryptic and pained,
and read them to strangers
who could only follow up to

the sea. Meanwhile the island
floated away, or so it seemed,
more distant each time I pulled
at memory's oars, the color
of its currency changing, its
slang, its rumors, the music

behind its masquerade. Once
a year, I jumped behind them,
pulling at their dominoes,
hinting at my condition, and
everyone just waved, welcoming
or chasing. My step had changed,

I had been to Rome and
done as the Romans, I had
pushed the door to the factory
and smelled the sweat of the slave,
and I was returning to
the field of cane burning after

what could be the last harvest.
I am picking my way among
the ruins of the small capital,
the clocks that grew too large
for its shelves, to salvage
myself, to start over.

II. Casualties

Don't Go Home

They all know you there. Go to
Italy instead, or the South of Spain.
A villa is 300 a month, and the maid
will do more than clean.

Don't go back to that island
where bandits are just waiting for you,
and the claustrophobic hills
will stifle what voice you have left.

Go further away, learn new languages,
test the Mediterranean's cobalt
against the blue you've known
since childhood, row till your boat

bumps up against the shoals
of an unfamiliar shore. Let your lines
snag on their minarets, even as you arrive
on a day of unrest, while people

are busy ducking. Ah, but you won't.
You'll go back to that tiny savannah,
its missing racetrack, the pools
of little fish in the hollows,

and you'll run, like those nuts
ahead of the bulls in Pamplona,
through the narrow streets
of Port of Spain.

Entering the City

There was a man who begged on the streets
of Baghdad unaware there was a war, until
he saw the tanks crossing the Euphrates.
Then he began to drag himself across
the Street of Lamps, screaming to Ali
the shopkeeper to let him in. But before
he could pull himself up to the pavement
the rubber tread of the first vehicle loomed
close to his eye, and the dust-covered metal
ground down, first on his hand, then
on the rest of his torso, such as was left over
from the last war. And the driver
thought he had heard something, but soon
forgot the sound, as his gunner scored
direct hits, on one dome after another
of the city they were sworn to liberate.

The March

Red flags, banners, raised fists-
they're coming down the avenue
singing workers' songs.
The police are following close behind.

They're marching four abreast,
the young ones doing a dance,
a chance to be seen, the cameras
moving up and down the ranks.

The onlookers hear the 'C' word
and say, not me! They take the free
newspaper with the crowded print and
leave it on the first convenient counter.

We find them eccentric, these folks
who live in integrated areas near factories
and call each other comrade, and exchange
clothing, and baby carriages.

Their names are on file with the FBI.
Their candidates get two percent
of the popular vote. We're convinced
that they're on the wrong road,

people who claim a worker's right
to a fair day's wages for a day's labor,
and the right to say the family of man
has to have a hand in the sharing of the corn.

Casualties

In human terms, the cost is high.
The earth will have to dig in her purse
like an old woman or the butcher
will take back his meat.

Perhaps it's not so bad. She can wrap herself
in leaves and eat the tomatoes
that burst their thin skins. She can squat
near palaces in cities built of her own clay.

She can follow the armies that take her dirt
to bury their dead. She can swallow her pride,
pockmarked and disguised as a refugee,
she can sit in a camp. Or, a pretty blue marble,

she can smile in the eye of one whose hobby
is astronomy, spinning with her sun and moon,
sucking salt
through a wooden spoon.

A Well-Bred Woman

She leaps to her feet
condemning the cops
who shot her son.

She turns into something
primitive, screaming
the American word

for a man
who sleeps with
his mother.

She puts her hand over
her mouth as she hears
the keys rattle as they

are let out to walk free
on the grass outside
the courthouse where

no lion waits
to eat them, though
she prayed for one,

no owl hooting
at the noonday sun,
no calamity like

a building waiting
to fall
on the black sedan

that drives away
with them
down the highway.

The reporters ask and
she tells them, Amadou
is a common name

in my country, it is
like stones on the road,
and there are many

fathers named Diallo,
who all rush out when
they hear the drums

saying your son
your son your son
Amadou. They look

everywhere, in the home,
in the compound,
in the cassava fields

down by the riverbank
where the crocodiles
steal the goats,

they search until
they remember the one
who went to America.

Then they hug
the remaining Amadous,
and weep.

Stiff Upper

In a kiosk selling papers the Indian
ducked when the first bomb went off.

In the smoky exit from the tunnel
a policeman bled from one ear and

changed his radio to the other.
In Hyde Park for the moment

the speaker forgot what he had to say,
as into one of the offices of Immigration

a pigeon flew, scattering forms.
And then the bus,

O, the bus bound for Piccadilly
made an unprecedented leap

across the intersection, the conductor
stern-faced in the open air, the roof

blown off, all of England
bloody well blaming the Irish before

they thought about it a minute, that
that had been another war.

Modern Myths

Great snores come from the olive grove
where a giant tortoise is having
his dream of the sea. It shakes the cities and

makes LA think there's an earthquake. Meanwhile
a motorist is snaking his way to La Jolla
looking for a place to hole up for the night.

A girl is walking home alone, her man gone
to Tijuana with a dark-skinned slut
whose drawers showed when she danced.

From here the land stretches to the border,
Arizona asleep under the stars, the saguaro
praying someone will come along

who believes a hug from a cactus can be
soothing. In a joint where they serve ribs
as thick as a man's forearm

they keep John Wayne's six shooters
in a sparkling display case, next to his spurs.
And they square dance while

up the road in a cardboard shanty Geronimo
waves his tomahawk, yelling
the Apache word for war.

Syl and Stella

He wrote her saying
the coins were beginning
to weigh heavy in his pockets.

And she remembered that whenever
she'd ask for carfare, he used to
give her all the change he had.

So as soon as she received that letter
she packed and took
the next flight home.

III. WALKING BACKWARDS

Resources

Come up to the guard rail
and look into the lands below:
those hot and simmering lakes that
bubble in answer to your murmurings.

Kurtz beckons you to jump, but don't.
Take your pictures and send them
to your loved ones, write
'Wish you were here, the asphalt fumes

make us fall in love with death.'
Come no closer than a circling bird,
its feathers hardening before the fall,
and make a recording of its screeches

that end in the dictionary of fossil and ruin.
And read the sign tacked to the bridge
where they weigh the sealed barrels
of excavated tar:

No visitors beyond this point.

Tar Pit

This dark lake of crude
is our good fortune to have,
and get good money in return,
and magical stories to tell,

how a giant lies sleeping
on the bottom, his feces
black as pitch, and the gas
he emits is the discovery

that fills our pipelines.
The oily pools that dot its surface
are healing baths of his urine
that whiten the skin, and

the occasional bone is
of a cow he has not digested,
whose dna once tested
might prove to be human.

This is how the grown-ups
frighten the children of La Brea,
pointing out black footprints on
the stairs, and roads soft and sinking.

Sando Proper

for Dawad

No time now to change the name
the city was born with. The souvenirs
are printed, hundreds of them, and
streets are well known, looking down
from the hill.

The ocean laps in a count that soothes
the drunk at the bar. Change it now,
move his stool one inch and he will
lose the point he was making.
The taxis idling against the wall

know the dip and angle,
the canefield outside the town
sends its shadow back to the rock
as the cane stands waving, and when
they light it the ash has its own

way of descending. More than once
they started to build over, tried
to level the land to include the gulf
in every view, shanty and
mansion, gate and gallery.

But Lord Street and High Street
wouldn't stop slanting to the sea,
and the heart of the city claimed
the word 'Proper', though no one
could ever find it.

So the outlying districts formed
a circle, and the oil that bubbled
made the invaders keep coming,
ordinary barbers stropping razors
as if for war. And when

the promoters announced fetes
at Palms, and other outings, who
swung high in the air and kissed
her darling? The town that told
Port-of-Spain men, no, the lady's
not dancing.

Black Indians

Hungry the ocean devours the land,
pitting British against Spanish.

Guarahoons in hats shaped like ships
come ashore near the mouth

of the Nariva, the natives
not recognizing their own cousins

until they remove the black beads
from their noses.

In a museum by the pitch lake
the hull of Sir Walter's boat sits,

the voices of those who let him sail
drowned out by those who would have made

a teacup of his head. On Carnival Day
in single file the masqueraders reenact

the stories of conflict, mother-of-pearl
falling from their singlets, fishnet

converted into stockings, in their purses
fistfuls of gold

to buy back the souls of sailors
still stranded on the open sea,

the buoys in the Bocas tinkling
like bells at dinnertime.

Evening at Carenage

There are not many bathers
this evening, a few small families,
the children's
noises contained,

the littlest ones running
at the first boisterous wave
to solicitous aunts,
one of whom

in a bright blue suit
rescues a tumbling child,
scolding the rest
for their inattentiveness.

But he, even as he stutters
and hides his face,
before she can complete
her concerned embrace,

ducks and runs to welcome
the next surging line of foam,
the others falling
in a heap of helpless laughter.

Crusoe's Kin

I walk the longest beach in the world,
tracing the shape of outcroppings
against the horizon, logging the miles
with my feet in the sand.

I send messages,
using a shell to receive and transmit.
The fish intercept and come in
like armies, fins raised and ready.

I wave them back. These are
mistakes of the imagination.
The great ocean is still pounding,
water swirling in eddies and pools.

I pace back and forth
inventing the danger
around the next promontory
and under the sea,

where cables lie fat
with muffled long distances,
and crabby operators somehow
avoid the net.

The Careening Poui

for Dionyse

In dry season her blossoms spring to life.
Butterflies play in her hair
and lovers claim affinity.

Like a madwoman out of St. Ann's
spreading her bright skirt she laughs
as we mutter our problems.

As we crash our cars along the highway
she holds a stately line along the median,
bowing behind ambulances.

She wears pink bloomers,
changing to yellow as she climbs the hills.
She behaves badly,

an innocent, an exclamation
of love, crazy
as a flower can be.

Telling Time

So chimes the old clock once for
quarter, twice for half, and the time
by the old Indian you ask is about
right. Nothing is as loud as

the stillness of the savannah at noon.
Unless a storm breaks suddenly
you can hear the spokes of heaven turning,
the gossip of grass, the flamboyant

putting out new flowers. This
is where you'll sit with the mind out
of office, the air warm and tasting
of something curative.

You'll come here, eventually, after
a long absence. The girl whose hand
you held, the kite you flew, the hour
you know now like the Indian, by heart.

Jockeys

The horses bunch
as they approach the McCarthy Bend
where many stumble and fall.

As they go into the straightaway,
the gray mare with blinders
takes the lead and suddenly,

I find myself trapped in her gaze,
carried like those smallest of men
who weigh hardly anything at all.

Open Savannah

You don't have to find
an opening in the rails now.
You can saunter in, newspaper
underarm, the cannonball blossoms
dropping like stink bombs,

and go in and out of
the paddock, the spirits of
horses neighing their names
in the white air of morning,
the practice track ghostly with
spumes of sand,

and trace the path where
a man greased from head to foot
once crawled on his belly
to rape a woman, her companion
running to find the police station
in the dark.

You can still hear her whimper
at the threat to cut her throat,
The tick of tires in the traffic
radiating from that spot
as the sun rises to reveal
the shell of a precinct
and its condemned cells.

You can drag your feet on the
still-wet grass to wipe away
the memory's slime, and run
between the goalposts at both ends
of a soccer field, your boots
making new marks in the dirt.

But the scene is
hard to erase: the tiny cemetery,
the three straight palms, the kite
that keeps zigzagging its tail
of typewriter ribbon no longer
in use anywhere.

Agouti Look-Back

The savannah was always
one of the favorite places
to make love.
They could be seen going,

a man with a rolled-up newspaper
in his back pocket, the woman
walking ahead, pretending
not to be with him.

The house of a thousand bedrooms,
they called it. Though it was
dangerous, and things came
crawling through the grass,

people took their chances.
And in the morning a customer
might be heard telling
one of the cooks at the Breakfast Shed

a story about
the old agouti look-back
last night, in that most
public of places.

The Ordeal

Somehow she managed to untie herself
and make her way through the forest
until she reached a road where
a driver stopped and picked her up.

"They burned me with cigarettes,"
she said, "they buried me in a hole."
Back in the bush the kidnappers quarreled
about who was supposed to watch her.

They buried the rope and the duct tape
and the corned beef cans. They separated.
One went home and
the other two hid in the city.

The villagers sheathed their cutlasses
and talked about what they would do
if they found them. Her father looked
around, as he entered his yard.

The mother rose from her knees
before an altar in the bedroom
when the girl said she'd heard growling,
and saw the eyes of animals everywhere.

Cascade

for Leroy

On his veranda we listened to
the author's tale of two agoutis
that crossed the river that morning,
in the background the sound of
water dripping.

We were attempting, in one shot,
to resolve questions of governance
and will, right-of-way and ownership,
the language that lingers after disaster
when we surprise ourselves by being
still among the living. We talked

about the dog that survived the tsunami
by riding a mattress, the old man who was
squirted from the sewers into the sea,
while our host slipped some sort of
nutmeg extract into our chocolate,

and the ravine continued to murmur,
the bamboo rafting in dips and rises.
The demitasses shook, the cd ended,
and the novel sat under the hand of the man
who set it, ink still wet, title tentative.

The Dinner

The chairs scrape as the guests
sit for dinner.

The chatter is light, the dishes clatter,
 the oysters shine in their shells.

The guest of honor smiles to be
in this company. Beyond the walls

the university, half-empty, waits
for September. Soon the topic turns

to the rash of robberies in the area,
what the country is coming to.

In the driveway that circles to the door
the men on duty don't hear

the gravel crunch underfoot until
the intruders are upon them.

The dinner guests rush to the window
at the sound of gunfire.

They see the bodyguard
on the ground,

his blood like dark sealant
leaking from the car.

They call the police who are slow
in coming to take the ex-president

to safety, to cordon off the hills before
the murderers could make their getaway.

This Island

This island used to ring
with the shouts of children
playing

This island used to laugh
with its face and hands
up to the sky

This island used to be
content with the sea lapping
at its sides

Now this island is strange
with its sun stinging like ants
its night encased in shadows

This island is reeling as if
from a blow to the temple
it staggers about

This island sleeps in its squares
and plays in its too too
and asks why

This island calls its children
inside, and follows them
to school and back

This island begs for its life
and offers money, this island
spends money on foolishness

This island has money to burn
this island takes money under
the counter it markets its goods

it fishes for drugs
and pockets its revenues
and litters its shores

this island spouts bitumen and
cannot pave its roads, its sidewalks
a blind man's hell

This island dreads the gunman
and runs home at six   this island
is homeless and needs a bath

This island is awash in blood
and floods every time it rains
This island is drowning

For Carnival this island
dances up a storm and shows
its behind to strangers

This island drinks
rum and gramoxone and drives
by blowing the horn

This island cries mercy
to the god they say
lives in the mountains

and keeps out hurricanes
It looks to leaders who
will not listen   who

roll up their windows
and drive away   this island
wants them to come to the villages

and see the damage done
when the toxic drums blow up
this island wants a new courthouse

This island keeps the hangman
waiting while it slowly
sentences itself to death

It can't decide what to do
about anything   it wont stop
until it is finished and wherever

the flamboyant's in bloom
this island appears to be
burning

Hard of Hearing

They tell me it's raining hard
in the island now. This is good,
you would think, after such a dry spell,
people would stand and drink.

But they complain it's too much,
umbrellas are useless, shoes are soaked,
and there's not enough camphor
to still the wheezing.

And when the sun comes out
so hot it scorches the skin it
plays a crazy song
on the galvanize.

Fowls swoon, and the blood
feels like it's turning to steam.
They are waiting for Sunday, when
the light grows softer, the radio

plays hymns all day, and converts
tilt bravely backward into the font,
risking deafness, like Audrey ever since
going "Eh? Eh?" And still no answer.

Lisa, Look

for Tony McNeill

It's ten years now
since he died and I still
hear his query: Mervyn,
which you think is better,
Lisa look, or Lisa see?

I can see him now, smoking
in the fore-day darkness of
the house at St. Ann's, typing
without ribbon, using a lighter
to see behind the carbon paper
the washed-out blue words,
tiptoeing into the bedroom
to ask his mother's opinion.

"Good God," she'd exclaim, but
softly, when her patience ran out,
"Who's the poet, Tony, me or you?"
And sheepishly he'd go back
to pounding, but lightly, so as not
to wake anyone, same reason
he wouldn't turn on the light.

In the morning he'd invite me
to go for a swim. I'd been warned
about his driving, how
he'd converse and take his hands
off the wheel. Which he would do
as we went along, on and off
the road, picking up a girl,
asking her what she thought of
his seven-page unfinished poem.

We'd sit on the sand and
he'd put his flippers on, resting
his typewriter and papers
on his towel. I'd watch him
disappear into the sea, and
eventually appear
at a rock too far to call out to.
How deep inside himself he was,
how unreachable by anything
except poetry!

"Listen," he advised me. "Shit
on your enemy's porch. That way
they learn to leave you alone."
Dripping, he'd bend over his work,
lighting up in the strong wind
and clacking away, the words
printing on my ear
though there was nothing on the page

until he peeled it back,
and the poem *For Lisa* sprang out,
finished, spreading its light
the length and breadth
of Runaway Bay.

Cumana

The day will come
when I'll never see
this ocean again.

So I drink it in,
from the cup of my body
to the soles of my feet.

I share it
with the lady
at the fish stall. She too

begins to wonder
who will be here, what
will cover this ground.

Suddenly a swell comes
from some disturbance
in the deep.

By the time it reaches us,
mere bubbles whispering
to the sand, Joyce

(that's her name)
has fried two pieces
and tamed the sea.

Umpire!

What a lovely picture
the cricketers make against
the evening in their whites,
the commentator describing them
in sibilant phrases as the sun
descends slowly.

From the police barracks
Serpentine Rd. wanders into
St. Clair, between the mansions
among the trees, where me
and Mellie used to make love,
the occasional corporal going
about his business.

Back in those days there were
more peeping toms than rapists,
more groping than sex. We heard
coming from the oval the fans
arguing over Ganteaume's
ninety-nine singles, and
Constantine's catch that saved
the governor's head.

Now there's a slight breeze
blowing from the pavilion end
and the players are having tea.
When play resumes we
will try to score in what little time
remains, before appealing for light.

IV. Namesakes

Asking

A man comes to the fence and inquires,
Who lives here? He is looking for my uncle,
who has been dead some fifteen years now.

"I'm a musician," he says. He has been
playing the cruise ships, and expects to
again in September. He has heard, since

he was a young man, about Syl Taylor, the
great calypso entrepreneur, and hoped
one day to meet him. He moves toward the gate.

"May I come in," he asks, his hand upon
the latch. Immediately the dogs in the back
start barking furiously, and I wave him away.

No, my uncle is dead and there is nothing
to tell about his business. Besides, who comes
to inquire about a legend so long after, who

gives out addresses and information to strangers?
This is a time when people speak kindly then
tie you up, and put their hands in your pockets,

or worse. I tell the children to come inside, I
sit in my uncle's favorite chair and watch the man
go slowly up the street, looking over his shoulder.

Going Home

for Winston Harrington

I hope the plane isn't crowded
when he travels so he can stretch his legs
across three seats, and I hope
that nice girl I met when I went home
is working the flight, so she will let him have
as many cushions as he wants and fix him
a meal of only the soft stuff that he eats now,
and smile that pretty way of hers
that even his wife won't mind,

and I hope the pilot is one of those exceptional
BWee guys who make it seem so easy
you hardly know when you take off and land,
just a soft bump as you taxi in, who make
small talk for the whole trip in the parlance
Harry loves, saying, instead of turbulence,
"We just have to make a little giddy in de hole"
so all the passengers laugh, and feel comforted,
and raise their behinds and crane their necks
so they can see each other.

And when they land I want the sun to be
shining, or if it's drizzling lightly
for a rainbow to appear by the flyover, and
his grandson to be chatting incessantly all
the way home to his house in Turn Back Alley,
and the breeze to be just laden with the heady
smell of ladies of the night, though it's only
afternoon. And his wife and daughter to
stand on either side of him with their hands
under his arms, and hold him up so he can look

over the rooftops down to the sea, so the view
will enter his eyes and go straight to his heart,
stepping over the dog that lies sleeping nearby.
Then the steel band just below will begin
practicing a tune he's never heard before,
and he'll forget all about where he's been,
the whitecaps rising and falling with the music,
the arranger striking for them to stop
and take it from the top once again,
only faster this time.

Now!

for Harry

The night of the big blizzard he said
he couldn't wait any longer and
took off. I could hear him quoting
classics under the ceiling of the sky.

I called and called through the cloud cover,
as snow smothered the world and his wife
danced him like a baby in her arms,
a baby with white hair that had turned

as straight as an Indian's. Last night's
full moon shone dumbly here, but there,
through the tropic window where he lay
taking smaller and smaller breaths,

it grew big and urged, Take him, he has to
go now, to see the sea and hear the pan,
to scale the boundary of his property.
And this morning as she came in

Rosita noticed how his hand kept
reaching for hers, as if he were ready
to jump, and had already put on his socks,
and was just waiting for her to say when.

A Betting Man

When he can't be found at the government office
where he works Harry's at the betting pool,
picking Jetsam in the second to win, or
Crazy Ursula to place.

He's close to retirement, so no one complains.
His top drawer overflows with torn-up tickets,
and what little work he's been assigned goes
to the new clerk, who learns as she goes along.

He likes the one on Henry St., where they know him,
his white hair stark in the dim parlor,
his eyes steadfastly on the screens. For lunch
he hops over to the restaurant on Charlotte,

a card game going in the back. He has a chat
with his teacher friend, an expatriate returned.
They scold each other about bad habits, then hurry
before the next hand is dealt, the next race run.

He picks his horses as he does his friends,
with blinders on. He likes whom he likes, never
bets on strangers. Never mind who's riding
Crazy Ursula, Harry goes with her all the way.

The Bronx, Trinidad

That's the club at the top of Henry St., where
the boys swap stories of New York when they ran
with the uptown gang, and Miley fell from a roof
running from the cops, and Thelma was always
planning to come back home, but never made it.

Her funeral was in one of those Spanish parlors
under saints with garlands of plastic flowers. When
Wendell heard the wailing from the chapel next door,
he went through the wrong entrance, ending up
among the Latinos. The boys never let him forget it.

Now living in the island again for whatever reason,
they sing calypsos from way back when, and keep
traces of the American twang for whenever friends
come down. They wear caps with the NY logo,
inspecting the girls with a curious leer.

There was a boat in the harbor taking on crew,
is how they explain leaving back in '45, headed
for places like Mobile and Galveston. From there
they just kept moving till they hit where the accent
was familiar, and somebody had a basement

round Kingsbridge Rd. There was a numbers joint
on the corner, what you call whe-whe here. Teddy
had the spot up on Gun Hill, Cynthia was the waitress.
They look out at the staggered houses of Laventille
while talking like this, stump of a cigar in a corner

of the mouth. What makes a man stay away so long,
what makes him return? This they stay quiet about,
the heat and the beer taking a toll. They rest their elbows
on the veranda rail and stare in the direction of the port,
somewhere beyond those old buildings, over there.

Walking by Lapeyrouse

One early afternoon
walking past the cemetery
I thought I heard my father say,
"Get out of the sun." I looked up
and saw the palms tall and still
over the tombs below, and I explained

I had promised a book to a child
whose father owned a shop
on the boulevard, and the hour
had come to me here, across
from the Government Printery,
an antique press in the front yard.

And as I turned onto that
wide street with the small houses
behind low walls, a girl walked
on the opposite side alone and
in white, coming from lessons,
carrying her books.
And she looked

neither left nor right, but
attended some thought that
shaded her from the heat:
there was about her something
removed from discomfort,
that went with her toward some
destination. And I moved

towards mine, where around
a table and two chairs three
children played, one to whom
the promise was made.
And the chorus of their voices
sounded above my father's,
and the rustle of the palms,
and the noise of the press
before it rusted in the sun.

Namesake

for Julian

My father, whose name you bear, wasn't given
to much company. I have to go to work
early in the morning, he'd say, putting on
his pajamas by six, and turning in.

He wasn't one to apologize for not
talking to the neighbors. First born, he
took after his father in gruffness, and
most looked away from his countenance.

But on his days off we rode the tramcar
like two school chums, and afterwards
sipped cokes in the café, and I asked him
about things, like the accident on the railway.

I knew there were some things
he couldn't tell me, that perhaps he wished
he had done differently, that for all
the pondering in his head

the world wouldn't change. I felt
almost as old as he was then, and wished I
had the strength to put him on my shoulder,
as he did me, as we walked up the hill.

The trams are gone, as he is too, the rails
taken up or overgrown. And the carriage
that took his thumb, gone with the rest
of the train, to destinations I never knew.

His Romance

It was crowded in the small bedroom:
The priest, like a robber behind the door,
Helen, the neighbor who had called me in,
and standing by his sickbed
my mother marrying my father.

He never opened his eyes; he lay still
while she held the hand that fell on the covers
the moment she let go. And when they proffered
the document for him to sign he looked up as if
only just becoming aware of us in the room,
and wrote, his fingers awash in the gold of the afternoon.

Picture of a Man at Peace

After my father died my aunt Sheila the Matron
sat him up in a rocker and had his picture taken.
A strong woman, I remember she took him bodily
from the bed, shunting his weight off her hip onto
the cane-bottomed seat.

His feet looked like feathers brushing the carpet
before she adjusted them, forcing them apart
until his heels rested on the crossbar as if he had
placed them there himself. He seemed to resist
as she pushed his head to one side, the way he
always grimaced when anyone tried to kiss him.

Except for Cousin Judy. Her he welcomed
and let smooth his hair and never bit, even when
she pried his lips apart to look at his teeth
which were strong and white till the day he died.
The rest of us he kept away from the money
stashed under his pillow, snarling
as the rheumatism took hold.

That's when Sheila came in her retirement
from Princes Town Hospital, her needles
blunt as screws, working them into his arm
while I watched, wincing as he winced, his skin
magnified by her glasses, folding under her bifocals,
till he screamed in pain.

Beyond that now, he sat, as the photographer
fixed the tripod and ducked beneath the black cover
to check the focus and the light. And I remember
how Sheila made him wait while she adjusted
my father's pajamas, and how in the snapshot
(that I could only bear to look at once),
they had come undone again.

Down the Main

for my mother

She came from a place
down the main
where old campesinos
sat drinking espresso

and gossiping about
the convent girls
and playing snooker
with short sticks.

She came from a village
where the priests
from Los Sanctos rectory
sang alarums, brown robes
sweeping the dusty streets,

down by the terminal
where the trams turned
in a shower of sparks
and wagged their way
back up the hill.

But she was a baby
and doesn't remember,
not even the orphanage
on a plot of land
overlooking the sea

that they say broke off
to form this island
in the shape of a shoe,
many, many years ago.

Uncle, Lately

Midmornings he lay there,
mouth open in sleep as if
he were practicing dying,
while the day went on without him,
the birds chattering, the leaves
shushing, the water
rushing down the drain.

And we walked more softly,
edging the house like lace, making
something soft to get him through
these hours. Or we stamped hard
to wake him. Then he shook,
startling himself, looking around,
slowly returning. Last week

we took him to a new doctor,
and he felt good all the next day.
Then that night he couldn't breathe,
and asked for his sweater,
though it was hot and humid.
Suddenly even standing
was a problem. The ambulance came.

His heart, his legs, his mind:
Well, he's eighty-nine, you know.
No appointment till February.
Someone said they set the date by
how long they think it will take to die.
We took him home and realized
he was shutting down

by sections, each part closing off
as the mind considered it.
His body was going dark,
the bells of workers jingling
on the evening road. One of them
was his own self as a boy,
happy he had found a job at last.

Masifé

Masifé, Masifé,
meet me down by the Croisée...

"Nobody comes to see me,"
the old man said in an interview,
though his exploits with women
had been many, and his battles
hard-fought and long.

"Nobody can stay. People
have planes to catch, others
to see. Sometimes we just
run out of things to talk about."
This morning he scalded his hand
making tea.

In that picture on the wall
he is handsome and strong.
He wore a long ponytail then.
He was about thirty, a champion
pool player, a fighter. Nobody
would believe he wasn't bad,
and just didn't like advantage.

Now it's all he can do
to keep his balance, put on
his shoes and go to get his pension
out on the main road where
someone might recognize him
and say, "Warrior, you still
moving good!"

Or some youngster
who doesn't know him at all
grab at his wallet and push him to
the ground. This morning he thought
a woman in the line looked familiar,

but when he smiled at her
she looked away, and the teller
calling "Next!" grew impatient,
and sucked his teeth, having no idea
who the old man was, or how
he'd come by his reputation.

My Brother the Boxer

He likes to see
if I can take a punch.
He folds his fist like a mallet
and hits me hard.

This is how he shows affection.
Sometimes he would spar with
a perfect stranger, right after
I introduce them.

We are two sons of a
left-handed woman, one wishing
he had the killer jab, the other
encouraging, poking at
the soft insides of his sibling,
feeling for the nerve
that *had* to be there.

Pediatrics

for Suchitha

The morning they called your name and said
you had met all the requirements you began
practicing your skills. You held the mortarboard
gently, retrieving it from among the others
where they fell. You brushed it off and handed it,
along with ribbon and certificate, to your mother,
who cradled it like it was her own.

A Lodging

Whenever we killed a chicken
the old Indian who lived under our house
would eat the heart and gizzard raw.

Though he only showered once a month,
he never smelled of anything but lavender.
One night we smelled smoke, and

heard him cough, a great rattle. And
in the darkness where he lay, each time
the breeze blew a shirt blazed

on the line strung over his bed.
Get out, my mother fumed at him.
From where, I wondered.

V. If Wishes Were Horses

Last Ones

for DW

Some fruits die on the branch,
birds sampling them at will,
while pickers curse the tree.

In storms some people
ignore offers of help, and
cling to chimneys, faith only
in stones they themselves cemented.

And when the landscape becomes
barren, blasted by the sea, such souls
can be found clinging to ropes
made of their own skin,

some great bird
whistling sweetly to the day
their names
in epics that go on and on.

Open Sepulchres

High winds blow our houses away,
flood waters take us down to the sea.
Criminals highjack us and leave us
standing at the roadside, shaking our heads.

We worked so hard for this belt
of safety, to avoid the wreck of hardship,
to fence off the field in which we lined
our plums all the way to the horizon.

Sad news always came from other countries:
the dust bowls, the hostage situations,
the nuclear meltdowns, the mad cows
running amok with disease.

We stacked our bricks till we could hardly
see anything, and counted the family,
making sure we had books to read
and love to last a lifetime.

But lately disasters come, some loud,
some sneaky, some from inside,
like a son with a gun,
while the second hurricane in a week

troubles our minds. Windows fly out,
shoes in the mud, hands in the air,
undoing the elements, knitting woes like
caps for the dead. O lining of life,

bulletproof paper, cells that flirt with
the invading cancer, operas of loss that
shatter the chandelier's blossom, we live now
in open sepulchres, bombs a bus away.

Something's Burning

The heat wave's over, at least for now.
They were bringing the elderly down
on stretchers all week to places called
cooling centers, where they served

Jello and reassured them they would
eventually return to their solitude,
once the mercury fell. In some states
they were keeling over like penguins,

the old codgers who insisted on
mowing their lawns, stiff as boards
in their bermudas, telephones ringing
in the dark interiors of their rooms.

Emergencies there are many
these days. It doesn't do to quarrel,
or search for answers. Just take
the damn flag and close the door,

the war, the heat, the hit and run
chasing down the highway like wolves
singed in a forest fire, howling like a cook
whose sleeve has caught the flame.

The Last Hubono

for Papa Antoine

The spirit gets up in the meeting, and steups.
Everyone has a pen at the ready, it will say
something important: the cutlass is not sharp
enough, the goat is getting away as we argue.

Sister Maude is as naked as she can be. Any
further under the spell and we cannot call her back.
Bam, she hits her head against the post, she breaks
loose from the chalk and makes her own marking.

The spirit sits on the step, conferring with itself.
It used to be easy to understand, when we remembered
the scrape and bow, the kick-up and buck, the sign
a crooked finger made above a rolling behind.

But now we must wait for Maude to return, her
virtue in a cup, her orisha dismounted and sleeping
in a tree. Like a jealous lover the spirit steups again.
Knowing a language is no good if you alone can speak it.

If Wishes Were Horses

I speak to the world in a no-nonsense tone,
"Stop spinning, you're making me dizzy,"
and it responds with a hurricane, forcing water
into my basement, blowing the cock off
my vane.

Go home, I say to the swarm of locusts
on their seventh excursion to my garden,
and the late-night crunching keeps me awake,
the house itself beginning to move
down the street like a leaf.

You customers at the shop of numbers, will you
never give up? There is no logic to the moon's
love of shadows. I fling my prayers upward
as you do the pieces of your lottery tickets,
and they keep going like horses, right

out of the savannah, through the city
to the edge of the swamp, where they
wake the sleeping ibises who ask
if there was anything else I wanted.

Everything in Quotations

Everything in quotations means
someone said it before, standing
in uncertainty as you are now,
believing the tide was close
to sweeping him out.

And as he blew dust
from some old page, the words came
from someone in the same predicament,
calling with such authority
it made the winds imagine
we could speak their language,

just as you could call out at this moment
from your sinking center something
you never said before, some pregnancy
with consonants like hot towels
ready to take it from you
and give to the next needy person:

a shout, as he turns and tells another
his story.

Prospects

The sun shines on the helmets of the cyclists.
A hawk watches a rat inching along the bike trail.
The policeman questions the young rider
about her binoculars. Yes, she's a birder.
There are about ten varieties of ducks
on this wetland.

Fall is a little ahead of itself, the hurricanes
chasing each other out of the tropics. Earlier
I met a man, a retiree like myself, running.
I have not yet run out of things to do. Still,
I can see it coming, the winter storm
when I'll stand at the window, looking out
at the snow. But for now

the swans are cocking their behinds
in the air, and each man has his running style:
Olympian, rabbit, turtle. The man I ran into,
a namesake, paced himself around an uphill turn,
favoring the leg that lagged behind. Recovering
from a stroke, he said, his speech slurring.

The hawk is keeping one eye on the rat. I can tell
it is about to make its move, which the birder
will miss, as most of us do, the moment
in our passion when the rise commences, chances
slim as catching the ducks in mating frenzy,
or that we will have this day to meet again.

Meanings

He's half asleep in the middle of the day,
like a man who has just taken a hard test,
and he's looking into the dark of his lids
for the number that would make the difference.
In English it was the topic that killed him,
the mongoose personified as a sly creature.

He was asked to give the setting, the year,
the exact moment when the composition
popped into the poet's head, and failing
that, to assume the point of view of a
giant rat, faster than a snake, a blur,
and the heat of the room overcame him.

So her whispering now, to accommodate
the slippage she felt, the loss of a child
they had not even attempted, was too loud
even for the newness of this romance,
her eye color only last night discovered
by accident as he bore down, a crick
in his back's rhythm. They were brown,
like a cricket's dry shade, and he had stopped
like the insect, listening for something.

Potions

After a tough campaign,
the politician drives by,
the loudspeaker gone
from the top of his car.

You can hear an orderly's mop
swish at the hospital,
the neighborhood has grown
so quiet.

O, what didn't the doctor do,
trained in his psychic, in
his meat and mental, the mind
swings back to childhood.

And in tropic waters there are
needles and things, needles
and things, and sick souls
come for the cure.

Fanfare

Let's turn tonight upside down
and find what was lost so long ago,
let's keep the corners moving and
look down the empty side streets
and into the traffic roaring.
Let's go into diners where
two or three sip their coffee slowly,
where the melancholy light plays on
blue muffins and our sparkling pins
as we come in
and run back out again.

Let's look up at the stars, the stars
that are there when we remember,
and run through the alley and burst
upon the thoroughfare holding our sides,
let's take a livery cab uptown, pacing
ourselves in store windows, yellow
lights and mannequins, until we don't
know where we are, like the river,
flowing north or south, and someone
calls out, hey lady, hey mister!

We're all grown up now; we can go
where we want, and stay as long.
Let's look in the water at our reflection,
and still as herons watch ourselves
turn silver as the sky behind us.
Let's go under the trees where shadows
still embrace and all together
let's lift the edge of night and find
the hollow of kisses, let's run through
it, turning the benches over and over.

Some Loves

An emptiness in the belly,
a burning near the heart:

symptoms of the moon
going down a dark valley
showing hardly any light.

Where does it hurt,
the doctor asks, and lovesick,
the sufferer points everywhere.

To See the Place

Among the many answers
given as reasons to travel,
Vera's was always,
to see the place:

Bright blazing lights, and
high waterfalls. Skyscrapers, statues
in stately parks, domed buildings
and gold minarets, marketplaces.

She marked them down in her mind
as seen, even the man flailing away
in a field, seen, and now part of
her body, her landscape.

And upon her return she'd answer
the silly question, why did you go?
a painted cart traversing her irises
for anyone who cared to look.

Remember

for EBT

If we meet again after this,
on some street corner,
or in a market place
in some foreign country

when the bombs
have stopped dropping
and you balance
a beautiful baby in one hand

testing melons with the other,
if we stand there in the hubbub
each staring and saying
how much the other has changed

or looks the same,
if I don't remember your name
as I introduce you to someone
who has befriended me and

stands patiently while we recall
days when the world
had gone crazy and you asked me
who would save it,

remember I said, you will,
even if I leave, even if you never
hear from me again, you'll
find someone to tell your story,

who will get word to the front
that the war is over and the children
can go back to the classroom now,
who will find me

wherever I am, in the mountains,
by the sea, waiting
and listening for the quiet
that will let us think, and when

we walk from each other,
you by way of the oranges, me
by the fish, my friend will look back
as I remember your name.

NOTES

NOON IN DAKAR
> *Bou-bou*: an elaborate Senegalese headdress.

SANDO PROPER
> San Fernando, a major city in the south of Trinidad, known for its hilly terrain.

BLACK INDIANS
> *Guarahoons*: a tribe of legendary ferocity, native to the coast of South America opposite Trinidad. They are a common theme of Carnival masquerades. *The Bocas*: A treacherous strait separating Trinidad and Venezuala.

THE CAREENING POUI
> *Poui*: plant native to Trinidad, with distinctive yellow or pink blossoms. St. Ann's: an asylum.

TELLING TIME
> *Flamboyant*: the flame tree. See also "This Island."

AGOUTI LOOK-BACK
> *Agouti look-back*: metaphor for a sexual position.

THIS ISLAND
> *Gramoxone*: herbicide popular for use in suicide. *Too too*: feces.

LISA, LOOK
> Anthony McNeill (1941-1996), Jamaican poet.

HARD OF HEARING
> *Galvanize*: zinc sheeting, used for roofing or fences.

UMPIRE!
> *Andy Gauteaume, Learie Constantine*: cricketers famous in their day.

GOING HOME
> *Bwee*: BWIA, Trinidad's national airline.

DOWN THE MAIN
> *The Main*: the Venezualan coast.

MASIFÉ
> *Masifé*: phonetic spelling of Mastiffe, the sobriquet of a legendaty badman. The epigraph is from an old calypso.

THE LAST HUBONO

Hubono: a high priest in the Rada tradition of West African religion as practiced in Trinidad. *Cutlass*: machete. *Steups*: sucking of the teeth, a sign of impatience or disgust.

Carenage, Cumana, Belmont, Port of Spain, Serpentine Rd., St. Clair, Turn Back Alley, Henry St., and Charlotte are places in Trinidad.

Ditmas, Roosevelt Island, Kingsbridge Rd. and Gun Hill are places in New York.